My World of Geography
LAKES

Angela Royston

Heinemann
LIBRARY

Young Explorer

www.heinemann.co.uk/library
Visit our website to find out more information about **Heinemann Library** books.

To order:
 Phone 44 (0) 1865 888066
Send a fax to 44 (0) 1865 314091
 Visit the Heinemann Bookshop at www.heinemann.co.uk/library to browse our catalogue and order online.

First published in Great Britain by Heinemann Library, Halley Court, Jordan Hill, Oxford OX2 8EJ, part of Harcourt Education.
Heinemann is a registered trademark of Harcourt Education Ltd.

© Harcourt Education Ltd 2004
The moral right of the proprietor has been asserted.

Editorial: Andrew Farrow and Dan Nunn
Design: Ron Kamen and Celia Jones
Illustrations: Barry Atkinson (p. 6), Jo Brooker (p. 9), Jeff Edwards (p. 5; pp. 28–9)
Picture Research: Rebecca Sodergren, Melissa Allison and Debra Weatherley
Production: Duncan Gilbert

Originated by Ambassador Litho Ltd
Printed and bound in Hong Kong and China by South China Printing Co Ltd

The paper used to print this book comes from sustainable resources.

ISBN 0 431 11791 8
08 07 06 05 04
10 9 8 7 6 5 4 3 2 1

British Library Cataloguing in Publication Data

Royston, Angela
Lakes. – (My world of geography)
1. Lakes – Juvenile literature
I. Title
551.4'82

A full catalogue record for this book is available from the British Library.

Acknowledgements

The Publishers would like to thank the following for permission to reproduce photographs:

Alamy Images pp. **18** (Ian Dagnall), **22** (Pictor/Imagestate); Corbis pp. **4**, **11**, **13**, **14**, **15**, **21** (Dave Houser), **23** (Dale C. Spartas), **26** (Joel W. Rogers); Getty Images/Image Bank p. **19**; Getty Images/Photodisc pp. **16**, **17**; Getty Images/Stone p. **25**; John Cleare Mountain Photos p. **8**; Michael Campbell Photography p. **12**; NASA p. **20**; Panos Pictures p. **10**; Photo Library Wales pp. **7** (Chris Gallagher), **24** (David Williams); Wilderness Photo Library p. **27** (John Noble).

Cover photograph reproduced with permission of Corbis/Ray Juno.

Every effort has been made to contact copyright holders of any material reproduced in this book. Any omissions will be rectified in subsequent printings if notice is given to the Publishers.

Contents

Some words are shown in bold, **like this**. You can find out what they mean by looking in the Glossary.

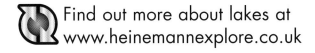 Find out more about lakes at
www.heinemannexplore.co.uk

What is a lake?

A lake is an area of water surrounded by land. Some lakes are small. Others are so big that you cannot see the other side.

This is Lake Arrowhead in California, USA.

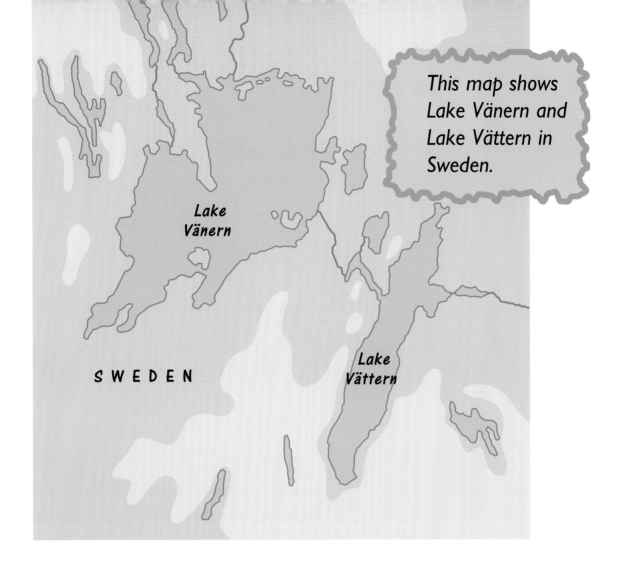

Lake Vänern

SWEDEN

Lake Vättern

Maps always show lakes as blue shapes in the middle of the land. Some lakes may look brown or green in real life, but they are always coloured blue on maps.

How lakes form

Lakes form when part of the land
is lower than the land around it.
The lower land makes a bowl shape.
Rainwater runs into the bowl and
fills it with water.

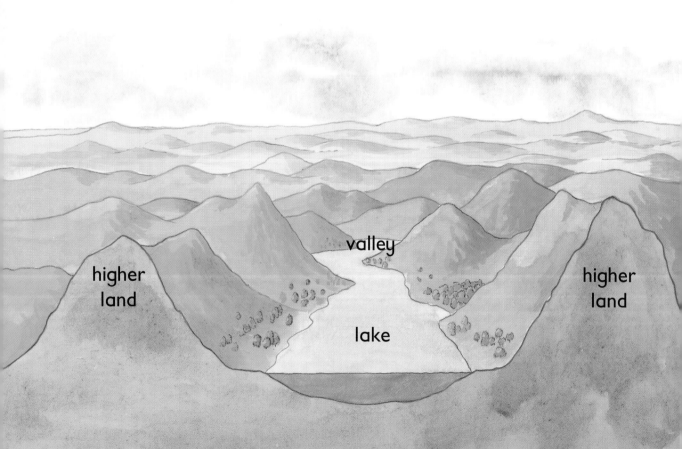

valley

higher
land

higher
land

lake

Many lakes form in the **valleys** between hills and mountains. Water runs down the mountainsides and keeps the lakes full.

Lakes and rivers

Most lakes are fed by streams and rivers that run into them. Most lakes also have a river or stream flowing out of them. This takes away extra water.

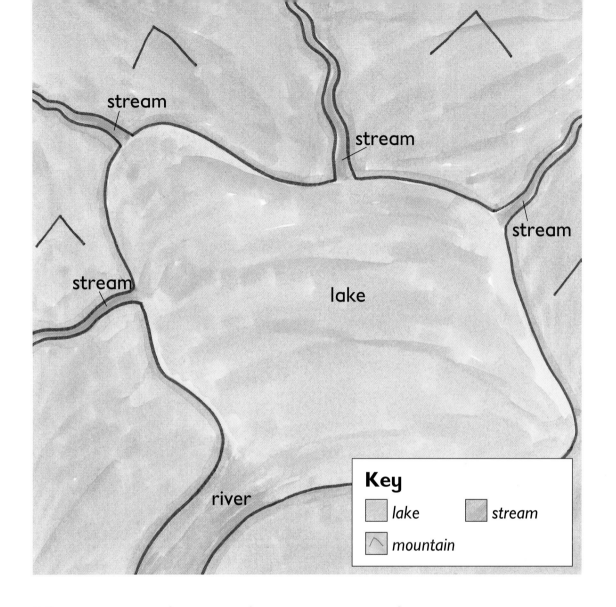

This map shows the streams that run into the lake on page 8. It also shows the river that flows out of the lake. You could draw a map like this.

Using lake water

People who live near a lake use the water in many different ways. Farmers may take water from the lake for their **crops**.

This crop is growing near Lake Titicaca in South America.

The city of Toronto is built next to Lake Ontario in Canada.

Many towns and cities are built next to lakes. Homes, offices and **factories** may use water from the lake.

11

Reservoirs

Sometimes people who live far away from a lake use the water stored in it. This kind of lake is called a **reservoir**. The word 'reservoir' means 'store of water'.

Water from
reservoirs is taken to
towns and cities far away.
It flows through pipes laid
under the ground. The water is
cleaned to make it safe to drink.

Dams

This is Glen Canyon dam in Arizona, USA.

A **dam** is a thick wall that is built across one end of a river in a **valley**. The valley fills with water to make a **reservoir**.

Special gates are sometimes opened to let some water flow through a dam into a river.

Sometimes a dam is built at one end of a natural lake. The dam stops most of the water flowing out of the lake.

Making electricity

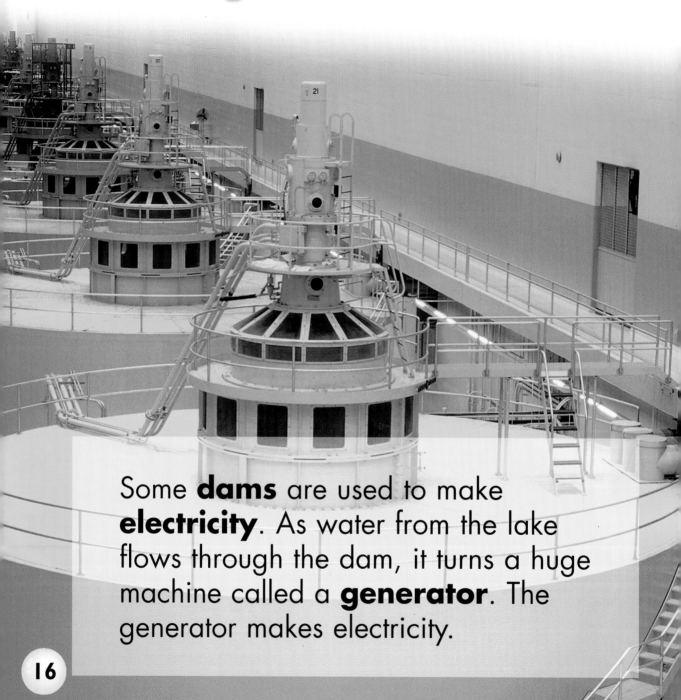

Some **dams** are used to make **electricity**. As water from the lake flows through the dam, it turns a huge machine called a **generator**. The generator makes electricity.

Electricity made by flowing water is called **hydroelectric power**. The electricity travels along electric wires to towns and cities far away.

Travelling on lakes

Travelling by boat is often the easiest way to get from one part of a lake to another. **Ferries** and **cargo** boats carry people, cars and **goods**.

Aeroplanes are a quick way to travel to and from lakes that are hard to get to. **Seaplanes** have **floats** so that they can land on, and take off from lakes.

Connecting lakes

The Great Lakes are five huge lakes in North America. Rivers flow from one lake into the next. The St Lawrence River joins the lakes to the sea.

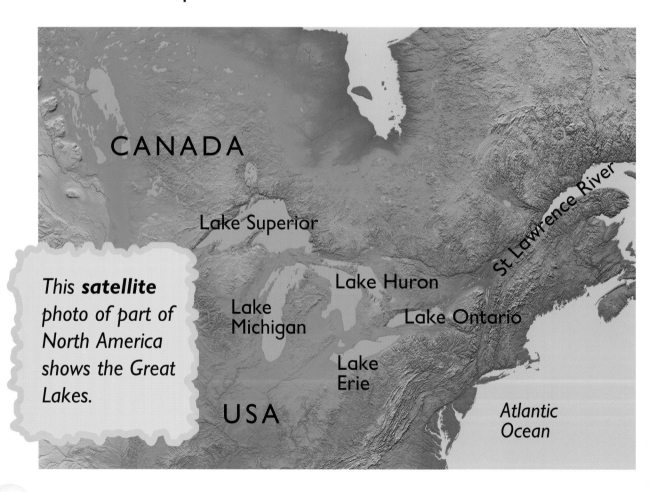

CANADA

St Lawrence River

Lake Superior

Lake Huron

Lake Michigan

Lake Ontario

Lake Erie

USA

Atlantic Ocean

*This **satellite** photo of part of North America shows the Great Lakes.*

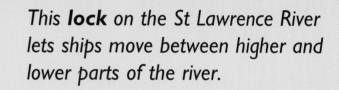

This **lock** on the St Lawrence River lets ships move between higher and lower parts of the river.

In North America, large ships sail from the Atlantic Ocean up the St Lawrence River to cities on the Great Lakes.

Fishing

Most lakes have fish and other water animals living in them. People who live near lakes catch some of the fish to eat.

These fishermen in south-east Asia are using cages to catch fish.

In some places, people catch the fish that live in the lakes for food. In other places, people catch fish for fun.

Enjoying lakes

Many people go to lakes for holidays and to enjoy themselves. In summer, some people go to lakes to swim or to fish. Others like to waterski, windsurf or use a **canoe**.

In some very cold countries, the surfaces of the lakes freeze in winter. Then people can skate on the ice. This lake is in the Netherlands. You should never skate on ice without an adult near by.

Protecting lakes

Lakes can easily be harmed. **Waste** from **factories** and homes can kill the fish and plants in lakes. People should get rid of waste in other ways to protect lakes.

If too much water is taken from a lake or **reservoir**, it begins to dry up. People should use less water, especially if the weather is very dry.

Lakes of the world

This map shows the biggest lakes in different parts of the world.

Great Bear Lake

Great Slave Lake

Lake Winnipeg

Lake Superior

Great Lakes

NORTH AMERICA

Lake Superior
Key fact: Lake Superior is the largest lake in North America.
Size: 82,100 sq km (31,200 sq miles)

SOUTH AMERICA

Lake Titicaca

Find out more about lakes at
www.heinemannexplore.co.uk

Lough Neagh
Key fact: Lough Neagh is the
                largest lake in the UK.
Size: 396 sq km
          (153 sq miles)

Lake Ladoga
Key fact: Lake Ladoga is the
                largest lake in Europe.
Size: 17,703 sq km
          (6835 sq miles)

Caspian Sea
Key fact: The Caspian Sea is the
                largest lake in the world.
Size: 371,000 sq km
          (143,250 sq miles)

Lough Neagh
Loch Ness

EUROPE

Lake Ladoga

Lake Geneva

Lake Baikal

Aral Sea
Caspian Sea

Lake Balkhash

ASIA

AFRICA

Lake Victoria
Lake Tanganyika
Lake Malawi

OCEANIA

Lake Eyre

Lake Victoria
Key fact: Lake Victoria is the
                largest lake in Africa.
Size: 69,484 sq km
          (26,828 sq miles)

Lake Eyre
Key fact: Lake Eyre is the largest lake in Australia.
                It contains water only for a short time each year.
                The rest of the time it is completely dry!
Size: 9583 sq km
          (3700 sq miles)

ANTARCTICA

Glossary

canoe narrow boat that you move by using a paddle

cargo goods carried by boat or plane

crops plants, such as wheat and tomatoes, that are grown for eating

dam thick, high wall at one end of a lake

electricity energy that is used to make light and heat and to make some engines work

factory place where people make things

ferry boat used to carry people and other things across a short stretch of water

float object that floats on water and helps a larger object to float too

generator machine that makes electricity

goods things that are made, bought and sold

hydroelectric power electricity made from flowing water

lock system that allows ships to move between lower and higher parts of a river or canal

reservoir lake whose water is taken in pipes to homes, offices and factories

satellite small object that goes round a larger object, such as a spacecraft going round the Earth

seaplane aeroplane that can take off and land on water

valley deep dip between two hills or mountains

waste left over materials that people do not want

Find out more

Further reading

Atlas One (Longman, 1994)

Make It Work! Geography: Maps by Andrew Haslam
(Two-Can, 2000)

Geography Starts Here: Maps and Symbols by Angela Royston
(Hodder Wayland, 2001)

Useful Websites

http://mbgnet.mobot.org/fresh/lakes/ – visit this
website to find out lots of information about lakes and animals
that live in lakes.

www.ace.net.au/schooner/mlakes.htm – this website
contains pictures and information about the Murray Lakes in
South Australia.

Disclaimer

All the Internet addresses (URLs) given in this book were valid at the time of going to press.
However, due to the dynamic nature of the Internet, some addresses may have changed, or
sites may have changed or ceased to exist since publication. While the author and the
Publishers regret any inconvenience this may cause readers, no responsibility for any such
changes can be accepted by either the author or the Publishers.

Index

Titles in the *My World of Geography* series include:

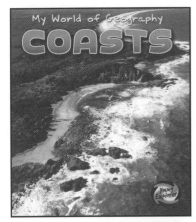

Hardback   0 431 11802 7

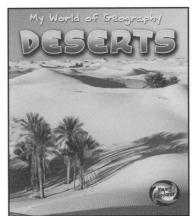

Hardback   0 431 11801 9

Hardback   0 431 11792 6

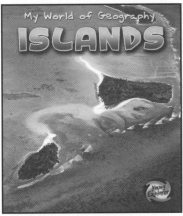

Hardback   0 431 11800 0

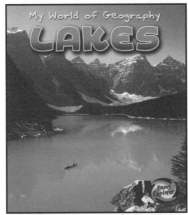

Hardback   0 431 11791 8

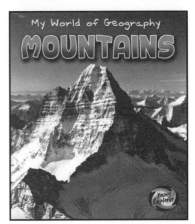

Hardback   0 431 11790 X

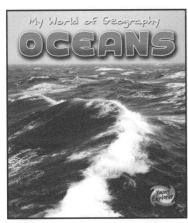

Hardback   0 431 11799 3

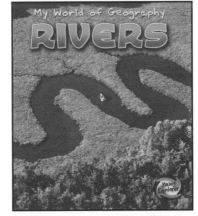

Hardback   0 431 11789 6

Find out about the other titles in this series on our website www.heinemann.co.uk/library